ORIGIN & MEANING

OF APPLE CULTS

ORIGIN & MEANING

OF APPLE CULTS

BY

J. RENDEL HARRIS, M.A., Litt.D., D.Theol., etc.

HON. FELLOW OF CLARE COLLEGE, CAMBRIDGE

ARABI MANOR
A REBEL SATORI IMPRINT

New Orleans & New York

Published in the United States of America by
Arabi Manor
A Rebel Satori Imprint
www.rebelsatoripress.com

Originally published by The University Press, Long,ams, Green &
Company, Manchester, United Kingdom, 1919.

*Reprinted from "The Bulletin of the John Rylands Library," Vol. 5, Nos. 1
and 2, August 1918-March 1919.*

Paperback ISBN: 978-1-60864-269-4

SARCOPHAGUS FROM VISCONTI: "MUSEO PIOCLEMENTINO," VOL. V., PLATE 16

ORIGIN AND MEANING OF APPLE CULTS.[1]

By J. RENDEL HARRIS, M.A., Litt.D., D.Theol., etc.,
Hon. Fellow of Clare College, Cambridge.

IN some recent investigations which I made into the origin of the Greek gods the suggestion was made that a number of the Olympian Divinities were personifications of or projections from the vegetable world. The plant or tree was first thought of animistically as being the residence of some virtue or potency, helpful or hurtful as the case might be, capable of being propitiated on the one hand, or employed in human service on the other : and it was not difficult to trace, in individual cases, the process of personification as the hidden life of the plant or tree became an animal form, a human form, or an ultimate deity. Amongst the cases which were discussed one of the most interesting was that of the great god Apollo, the lord of light and healing : it was suggested that the god was the personification of the healing virtue and solar attributes of the mistletoe, and particularly of the mistletoe as it is found growing upon the apple-tree ; and that the apple and its mistletoe are his original sacred symbols.

Moreover, since it is tolerably certain that Apollo in the Greek religion is a migration from the more northerly regions, and his mythical home is somewhere at the back of the North wind, it was not unnatural to suggest that the name by which he was known in the Hellenic world is not a Greek name at all, but itself a migration from some northern tribe : and it was audaciously affirmed that Apollo was only our apple in disguise.

One need not be surprised that such revolutionary views provoked sharp opposition. The religious conservatism of the scholarly world was offended, for scholars are still more pagan than Christian, and have never really lost faith in the more decent of the Olympian

[1] An elaboration of the lecture delivered in the John Rylands Library on 23 October, 1917.

deities. The degradation of the great god of light to a spray of mistle-toe, or to an apple-tree would have been blasphemy in ancient times, and is academic blasphemy still.

Even those who were not the victims of hereditary religious con-servatism found it hard to believe that there had been a northern apple-god, when no trace of such a divinity had even been detected, nor had any satisfactory parallel to Apollo turned up in the northern mythologies. It was not an unreasonable request, therefore, to be asked to produce one's apple-god in a definitely northern form, and to find the missing links between himself and our lord Phœbus. The object of the present lecture is to try and meet these criticisms and questionings.

CHAPTER I.

ON THE EXISTENCE OF APPLE CULTS.

ALL students of folk-lore are aware that, in collecting and comparing the quaint customs which still linger on the country-side, they are not merely dealing with customs, but with cults that underlie them, with misunderstood rituals and lost divinities ; in many cases the rituals and worships which are thus embalmed like flies in the amber of unchanging or slowly-changing popular habit, turn out to be the very earliest beliefs and the most primitive religious acts of the human race.   For example, it will not be easy to find anything that takes one further back re- ligiously or ritually than the Corn-baby, Corn-child, or Corn-mother of the harvest-field, of which so much has been written in recent years. Every surviving fragment of such a ritual is as valuable to us as a page of an early gospel which time has blurred, or whose first-hand has been overwritten.   We see through it, down a long vista across which many shadows are cast, the reasons which made man a religious animal, and not merely the superstitions that keep him so.   Of the customs of the corn-field there is not much more, perhaps, to be said ; the matter has had such exhaustive treatment at the hands of Mannhardt, Frazer, and others, that the field may be considered well reaped and satisfactorily gleaned, and there does not seem to be any last sheaf whose cutting might make the reputation of later investigators.   In the case of the fruit-orchard, the inquiry has not gone so far, nor been so effective.   If it should turn out, as we have recently suggested, that the ancestry of the god Apollo runs back into the apple-tree, in the same way as Demeter disappears into a peculiar bunch of corn-stalks, we can only say that Apollo was much more elusive than Demeter, and the identification of his origin is much more easy to contradict. Let us try to find out something more about apple-cults and the associated places where apple-sanctity has been recognised.   We will begin with our own country where there are traces of recently expired customs relating to the apple, which are in some respects parallel to those which occur, or used to occur until recently, in the harvest-field.

If we turn to Lysons' *Magna Britannia*, which is a storehouse of valuable observations of ancient customs, we shall find him describing practices which prevailed at a certain time of the year, in the orchards of Devonshire.   He tells us that :—[1]

" In most parts of the cyder-district a custom still prevails of what is called in ancient times ' wassailing the apple-trees '.   This custom was accompanied by a superstitious belief, in the words of an old poet (see Herrick's *Hesperides*),

> That more or less fruit they will bring,
> As you do give them wassailing.

This ceremony at some places is performed on Christmas-eve.   It consists in drinking a health to one of the apple-trees, with wishes for its good bearing, which generally turns out successful, as the best-bearing tree in the orchard is selected for the purpose.   It is attended by the singing of some verses apposite to the occasion, beginning ' Health to thee, good apple-tree '.   The potation consists of cyder, in which is put roasted apples or toast ; when all have drunk the remainder of the contents of the bowl are sprinkled on the apple-tree.   The old Saxon term ' wassail ' which is known to imply drinking of health is thus defined in the glossary of the Exmoor dialect : ' a drinking song sung on Twelfth-night eve, throwing toast to the apple-trees in order to have a fruitful year, which seems to be a relic of the heathen sacrifice to Pomona '." [2]

So far Lysons, who goes on to describe the cutting of the " neck " of the harvest in Devonshire, which we now know so well to be a tradition from the earliest strata of religion.   So we naturally ask how we are to interpret the wassailing of the apple-trees.   Is that also ancient ?   The use of the term " wassail " for the ceremony shows that it has come down out of Saxon times ; but there is much more in the account than can be explained by a Saxon habit of drinking health to everybody and everything at a particular time of the year.   It is clear that what the Devonshire rustics were engaged in was a veritable sacrament, in which they brought their deity to their deity and partook of their deity with their deity, under solid and liquid symbolism.

---

[1] Lysons, *Magna Britannia* (Devon), cccliv.
[2] Apparently this is from Grose, *Provincial Glossary*, 1790, *v. infra.*

Evidently we must try and find out some more about this interesting custom.

If we turn to Hazlitt's *Faiths and Folk-lore*, which incorporates most of the *Popular Antiquities* of Brand and Ellis, we shall find several accounts of apple-wassailing. We transcribe first an article on " Apple-Howling " :—

" In several counties the custom of Apple-howling (or yuling) to which Herrick refers in his *Hesperides*, is still in observance. A troop of boys go round the orchards in Sussex, Devonshire, and other parts, and forming a ring about the trees, they repeat these doggerel lines :—

> Stand fast root, bear well top,
> Pray God send us a good howling crop;
> Every twig, apples big ;
> Every bough, apples enou ;
> Hats full, caps full;
> Full quarter sacks full."

Hasted says :[1] "There is an odd custom used in these parts about Keston and Wickham (in Kent) in Rogation-week : at which time a number of young men meet together for the purpose, and with a most hideous noise run into the orchards, and encircling each tree, pronounce these words :—

> Stand fast root, bear well top ;
> God send us a youling sop,
> Every twig, apple big,
> Every bough, apples enow.

For which incantation the confused rabble expect a gratuity in money, or drink, which is no less welcome : but if they are disappointed in both, they with great solemnity anathematize the owners and trees with altogether as significant a curse." It is clear that we have evidence here, at least as far back as the end of the eighteenth century, when Hasted wrote his *History of Kent*, for the occurrence of some surviving ritual and magic in reference to the apple-tree.

Hazlitt continues : " It seems highly probable that this custom has arisen from the ancient one of perambulation among the heathens, when they made prayers to the gods for the use and blessing of the fruits coming up, with thanksgiving for those of the previous year ;

---

[1] No reference is given, but it is clear from what follows that he is quoting Hasted's *History of Kent*.

and as the heathens supplicate Eolus, god of the winds, for his favourable blasts, so in this custom they still retain his name with a very small variation ; this ceremony is called Youling; and the word is often used in their invocations."

Thus far Brand-Hazlitt on the custom of apple-howling. We need not spend time over Eolus ; he is certainly not the deity involved in the act of youling : the texts are clear for Yule-tide, and this again takes us back to Saxon times, and shows us that if the youling-custom was attached to Rogation-week, it has been transferred to it from the Christmas season. So we need not spend further time over the perambulations of the *Ambarvalia*, or the chants of the *Litania Major*. Incidentally we note that, as we are not deriving our apple-ritual from Rome, we may remove the reference which Lysons has given us to Pomona.

Now let us see what Hazlitt has to report elsewhere. Under the heading of *Twelfth Night* we are told that "formerly it was custom in Devonshire on this night to drink hot cyder and eat cakes, and after the company had partaken of this entertainment to their satisfaction, they proceeded into the orchard, where they offered a portion to the apple-trees and pear-trees by laying a piece of cake on a bough of each, and pouring over it a libation of hot cyder. The men who happened to be present then fired a salute, and the women and girls sang in chorus,

> Bear blue, apples and pears enou'
> Barn fulls, bag fulls, sack fulls.
> Hurrah !   Hurrah !   Hurrah !

There are several versions of the subjoined song : but that here given is correct in Devonshire on Twelfth Day :—

> Apple-tree, apple-tree,
> Bear apples for me :
> Hats full, laps full,
> Sacks full, caps full.
> Apple-tree, apple-tree,
> Bear apples for me.

" In the South-hams of Devonshire, on the Eve of the Epiphany, the farmer, attended by his workmen, with a large pitcher of cyder, goes to the orchard, and there, encircling one of the best-bearing trees, they drink the following toast three several times :—

> Here's to thee, old apple-tree,
> Whence thou mays't bud, and whence thou mays't blow!
> And whence thou mays't bear apples enow!
> Hats full, caps full!
> Bushel—bushel—sacks full,
> And my pockets full to!   Huzza!"

.   .   .   .

" On the Eve of Twelfth Day, as a Cornishman informed Mr. Brand, on the edge of St. Stephen's Down, 28 October, 1790, it is the custom for the Devonshire people to go after supper into the orchard, with a large milkpan full of cyder, having roasted apples pressed into it.   Out of this each person in company takes what is called a clayen cup, *i.e.*, an earthenware cup full of liquor, and standing under each of the more fruitful apple-trees, passing by those that are not good bearers, he addresses it in the following words :—

> Health to thee, good apple-tree,
> Well to bear, pocket-fulls, hat-fulls,
> Peckfulls, bushel-bag-fulls!

And then drinking up part of the contents, he throws the rest with its fragments of the roasted apples at the tree.   At each cup the company set up a shout."

This last reference appears to be taken from Pennant's *Tour in Scotland*.[1]

Now suppose we turn to Grose's *Provincial Glossary*, which is almost contemporary with Hasted (I quote from the second edition of 1790), we shall find, " Watsail.   A drinking song, sung on Twelfth-day Eve, throwing toast to the apple-trees, in order to have a fruitful year : which seems to be a relic of the heathen sacrifice to Pomona. Wassail.   Exm.," which concluding words I take to mean that *wat-sail* is *wassail*, and that the custom referred to is an Exmoor custom. Grose has probably taken it from a *Glossary of the Exmoor Dialect*.

We learn something fresh from this reference.   The custom is called wassail, and so is connected naturally (but not exclusively) with Yule-tide.   The throwing of toast must be noted, for it explains the line in Hasted's account, when prayer is made that

> God send us a good youling sop ;

i.e., a Yule-tide toast, as we shall see more clearly presently.   Pomona

[1] Ed. Chester, 1771, p. 91.

may be dismissed, and Yule has clearly the right of way against the howling Eolus, as already pointed out.

Now let us see whether we can get some further evidence as to the wassail-song and the wassail-customs in reference to the apple-trees on the Eve of Twelfth Day.

We quoted just now from Hazlitt-Brand a reference for apple-howling to the *Hesperides* of the poet Herrick. The passage is as follows :—[1]

> Wassaile the Trees, that they may beare
> You many a Plum, and many a Peare:
> For more or less fruit they will bring
> As you do give them Wassailing.

From this verse we learn several things ; Herrick may be taken as an authority for the West of England, and for Devonshire in particular ; the *Hesperides*, which, as its name implies, is a Western production, was published in 1648. So the custom of wassailing the trees pre-vailed in Devonshire in the middle of the seventeenth century. It was not at this time limited to apple-trees, but was a general charm to make all fruit-trees prolific in the coming year. The name of " wassail " by which the custom is covered goes back naturally to Saxon times.

It is interesting to notice the modification of the word in country districts where it was no longer understood. In Mrs. Latham's *West Sussex Superstitions* we find the following statement :—

" It is the custom in the cider districts of Sussex to *worsle* the apple-trees on New Year's Eve, and for several succeeding days, and it is considered unlucky to omit doing so." [2]

Here *worsle* is a debased form of *wassail* in Sussex dialect. Ap-parently, in some parts of Yorkshire, the term *wassail* was corrupted to *vessel ;* for it is said that " it was usual to carry about the *vessel-cup* at Christmas, and sing carols, with a view to collect money. This was done in 1813, and perhaps later, at Holderness and in other parts of Yorkshire. The cup was sometimes accompanied by *an image of Christ and roasted apples*." [3]

We shall see presently that the roasted apples are properly a part of the ritual of wassailing the orchard, and it is significant that an image

---

[1] Ed. Moorman, p. 264.
[2] Quoted also in *Folk-Lore Record* (1878), 13.
[3] Hazlitt-Brand, p. 620.

of Christ is carried in the procession.   Does this belong to the wassailing of the trees, or is it merely a reminiscence of Christmas generally ?
At all events the roasted apples should be noted, and the disappear-
ance of the ancient word which covers the ceremonies.

To return to Mrs. Latham's account of the " worsling " of the
trees in Sussex : she continues :—

" Farmers give a few pence to the worslers, who form a circle
round the trees and sing at the top of their voices :—

> Stand fast root,
> Bear well top,
> Pray God send us
> A good howling crop.
> > Every twig
> > Apples big,
> > Every bough,
> > Apples enow.
> Hats full, caps full,
> Full quarter sacks full,
> Holla, boys, holla ! Huzza !

and then all shout in chorus, with the exception of one boy who blows
a loud blast on a cow's horn.   Last New Year's Eve the mother of a
sick boy told me that her poor child was sadly put out because he was
not able to *worsle* his grandfather's apple-trees ; and it is quite certain
that both mother and child expected a total failure of the apple-crop in
the grandfather's orchard to follow the omission."

We can add something to Mrs. Latham's account of the Sussex
ceremonies : a writer in *Notes and Queries* tells us that " in the
neighbourhood of Chailey (some miles to the north of Lewes) . . .
a troop of boys visit the different orchards," and after repeating the
chant before-mentioned, they " shout in chorus, one of the boys accompanying them on the cow's horn : during the ceremony *they rap the
trees with their sticks* ".[1]

In West Somerset they fire guns, apparently, at the trees : the
point should be taken in connection with the just-mentioned beating of
the trees with the sticks.   The whole custom for this part of Somerset
is described as follows :—

" On Old Christmas Eve (5 January), or the Eve of the Epiphany, it was the custom not long since, and may be still, for the

[1] *N. and Q.* (1852), 1st Ser., v., 293.

farmer, with his men, to go out into the orchard, and to place toast
steeped in cider, along with a jug of the liquor, up in the ' vork ' of
the biggest apple-tree, by way of libation ; then all say,

> Apple-tree, apple-tree,
> I wassail thee !
> To blow and to bear,
> Hat vulls, cap vulls,
> Dree-bushel-bag-vulls.
> And my pockets vull too !
> Hip ! Hip ! Hooraw !

(Bang with one or more guns.)   This ceremony and formula is repeated several times at different trees, with fresh firing of guns.   I can
well remember quite a fusillade from various orchards on Old Christmas Eve." [1]

There are very ancient features in this account which do not appear
in the customs of the Sussex villagers.   First and foremost there is the
presentation of the toast and cider to the biggest apple-tree in the
orchard, which is supposed to partake of the offering ; the ritual is
now turned into a communion service.

As we go further West we come across more traces of this curious
custom.

In Hunt's *Popular Romances*,[2] we are told with regard to the
" drinking to the Apple-trees on Twelfth Night Eve," that " in the
eastern part of Cornwall, and in western Devonshire, it was the custom to take a milk-pail full of cider, into which roasted apples had been
broken, into the orchard.   This was placed as near the centre of the
orchard as possible, and each person, taking a *clomben* [3] cup of the
drink, goes to different apple-trees, and addresses them as follows :—

> Health to the (*l.* thee) good apple-tree ;
> Well to bear, pocketfuls, hatfuls,
> Peckfuls, bushel-bagfuls.

Drinking part of the contents of the cup, the remainder, with the fragments of roasted apples, is thrown at the tree, all the company shouting aloud."

Mrs. Whitcombe in *Bygone Days of Devon and Cornwall* [4] tells

---

[1] Elworthy, *West Somerset Word-Book.*   [2] P. 175.
[3] *Clome* for *China* is still in use in W. Cornwall, or was in my early
days.
[4] P. 27.

the same story with slight variations : " They carry with them to the orchard a pitcher of cider and some cake. They hang pieces of this on *the branches of one of the trees, and sprinkle the cider over its roots.*"

It is further noted that " it is customary in some parts *to fire at the apple-trees*, and several guns are called into requisition for this purpose ".

Here the pieces of cake in the branches replace the toast in the primitive account. A special tree is the centre of the ritual, and our conjecture that the trees were actually fired at is confirmed. That the toast is actually soaked in the cider appears from the statement in Tozer's *Poems* that " it was the custom for the country people to sing a wassail or drinking song, and throw the toast from the wassail-bowl to the apple-trees, in order to have a fruitful year ".[1]

The general question of wassailing is summed up as follows by the editor of *Folk-Lore* in the year 1902 (pp. 95-6) :—

" The custom of wassailing and carrying a vessel-cup are noticed in Ellis's *Brand*, i., 1, 45 ; Henderson (2nd edn., 64-8), and *Gent. Mag. Library (Popular Superstitions)*, 16, 76. The information given may be summarised as follows : Wassailing, or health-drinking from a bowl or loving-cup was a usual accompaniment of Christian feasting, sometimes extended to the orchards and oxen. The favourite liquor was ' lambswool,' a mixture of ale, spices, and roasted apples. In many places parties of wassailers went about visiting the neighbouring houses singing their good wishes and carrying a bowl with apples, which the hosts were expected to fill with ale, or money to purchase it. But the custom of carrying a representation of the Madonna seems to have been confined to Northumbria, where the name ' vessel-cup ' and the apples are the only relics of the wassail-bowl which, one supposes, once accompanied it."

The writer did not get very far in his researches into the origin of wassailing, but he sees that the apples belong to the original function, and in the roasted form. How else could one explain the term " lambswool ".

Here is another small indication of the importance of the apple in the composition of wassail :—

" The Antiquarian Repertory (1775) contains a rude woodcut of

[1] Tozer, *Poems* (1863), p. 65.

a bowl carved on an oaken beam, which had formed a portion of an ancient chimney recess. The vessel rests on the branches of an apple-tree, alluding, perhaps, Sir Henry Ellis suggests, to part of the materials of which the liquor was composed" (Hardwick, *Traditions, Super-stitions*, p. 61).

Another point that comes up in the *Folk-Lore* Summary is the carrying of an image, this time of the Madonna in Northumbria. But here, again, we cannot assume that the image is an archaic feature of the ceremony, for the Yule-tide includes Christmas, and so the Madonna and the Christ may have come in on their own account, without any link with the sacred apple-tree.

It is likely that a good deal of confusion has arisen in the wassail ceremonies through the change in date of the Christmas festival from the Twelfth Night or Old Christmas Day (the Epiphany) to its present position. The wassail-bowl moved back when the date for Christmas receded, and the wassail-ceremony for the orchards remained on the old Christmas Eve. In modern times the wassailing date underwent, perhaps, another slight change in some quarters ; it was moved from Twelfth Night Eve to Twelfth Night itself ; here is a bit of West-country talk reported in 1908 : " Thicky Twelfth Night is not the hraight day for wassailing the arpul trees. Her should be doned on *Old* Twelfth Night, not on old Christmas Day," said the ancient sage of Stockland in January, 1908.[1] Apparently this means that the old West-country custom had moved forward a day.

There is, however, some evidence from Somerset that the wassail-ing of the orchards was moved back with the wassail-bowl, and perhaps the Christmas ceremonies, to Christmas Eve, and it may be to this that the aged rustic refers. Lysons, whom we quoted above, wassails the trees on Christmas Eve. In Poole's *Customs, Superstitions, and Legends of the County of Somerset*, 1877, pp. 6, 7, we find the following account of the Yule-log and the wassailing :—

" *The burning of the Ashen Faggot on Christmas Eve* is an ancient ceremony transmitted to us from the Scandinavians, who, at their feast of Yuul, were accustomed to kindle huge bonfires in honour of Thor. The faggot is composed of ashen-sticks, looped round with bands of the same tree, nine in number. When placed on the fire fun

[1] C. N. Whistler, " Sundry Notes from West Somerset and Devon," *Folk-Lore*, 1908, p. 91.

and jollity commence. . . . Every time the bands crack by reason of
the heat of the fire, all present are supposed to drink liberally of the
cider, or egg-hot, a mixture of cider, eggs, etc.   The reason why ash
is selected in preference to any other timber is, that tradition assigns it
as the wood with which Our Lady kindled a fire in order to wash her
new-born Son.   In some places it is customary for the yeoman and his
family to proceed to the orchard, one of the party bearing a hot cake
and cider, *as an offering to the best-bearing apple-tree*, and after
depositing the cake on the tree the cider is poured on the latter amid
the firing off of guns and pistols, the women and children shouting,

> Bear blue, apples and pears enough,
> Barns full, bags full, sacks full,
> Hurrah!   Hurrah!   Hurrah!"

Here again the Madonna appears to be an intrusion from the
Christian side, and the date of the wassailing has receded in accordance
with later Christian reckoning, but the ceremony itself is very archaic.
One tree stands out clearly as the object to be fêted, and it is difficult
to resist the feeling that the shooting of the guns is meant for the tree,
or for some representative of the tree.

In 1686 Aubrey published his *Remains of Gentilisme*, and in
this invaluable little book for the folklorist (it has been reproduced in
recent times by the Folk-Lore Society) we find reference to the wassailing of the apple-trees in Somersetshire.   Aubrey notes as follows:—

"Memorandum that *non obstante* the change of Religion, the
Ploughboies, and also the Schooleboies will keep-up and retaine their
old ceremonies and customes and priviledges, which in the West of
England is used still (and I believe) in other parts.   So in Somersetshire when the wassaile (which is on . . . I think Twelve-Eve) the
Ploughmen have their Twelve-cake, and they go into the Ox-house to
the Oxen, with the Wassell-bowl and drink to the ox with crumpled
horne, that treads out the corne; they have an old concerved rhythme;
and afterwards they goe with their Wassel-bowle into the orchard and
goe about the trees to blesse them, and putt a piece of tost upon the
roots in order to it."

Here we again have seventeenth century evidence for the custom of
wassailing the trees of the orchard in the West of England, accompanied
by a curious extension of the wassailing to the cattle.   Aubrey notes

that for the participation of the tree in the offering, the toast is placed, not in the branches, but at the roots. We had one case of this previously.

Similar results to our own have been reached by Mr. A. B. Cook, who has studied the legends in the Celtic literature with such astonishing industry and effect.[1] He finds out, in fact, from these legends, that the apple-tree was almost as sacred as the oak, that it had nearly as good a claim as the oak to the title *King of the Wood*, that on the one hand it represented the Sky-God, and on the other the life of a king or hero with whom it was associated. Mr. Cook suggests that the "religious or mythological transition from oak-tree to apple-tree corresponds to an actual advance in pre-historic civilisation. Tribes that were once content to subsist upon acorns and wild fruits in general learnt gradually the art of cultivating the more edible varieties of the latter, and so came in the course of many centuries to keep well-stocked orchards. . . . The apple in particular, the oldest cultivated fruit-tree in Europe, is felt to be the equivalent to the oak." The divergence between Mr. Cook's views and those of Dr. Frazer is not serious, it is a case of the expansion of an argument, not of its contradiction. Our own method confirms Mr. Cook's results from an opposite direction, *viz.*, the unnoticed survival of an apple-ritual, the centre of whose devotion was an apple-spirit.

At this point we may review the evidence which we have collected ; there would be more of it, but, unfortunately, my notes are lying somewhere at the bottom of the Mediterranean, and so we suffer from incompleteness at the hands of the war-god. Enough has been brought forward to show that we have unearthed a genuine ritual of which the apple-tree is the centre. This apple-tree, by preference the biggest or best or oldest of the orchard, and on that account entitled to be called (if the High Priest of Nemi will permit the appellation) the King of the Wood, is regarded as a sentient being capable of sacramental participation with its worshippers under two species : toast soaked in cider, with roasted apples form the one species ; cider, which is the life-blood of the tree, forms the other. The offering is shared between the divinity and the worshippers, and the offering is the divinity. Every side of sacrificial communion is here represented. The offering

[1] I refer to the papers on the " European Sky-God " in *Folk-Lore*, vol. xv., 1904, etc.

has an especial magical value ; it is a charm for fertility, and perhaps a reminiscence of previous fertility.   For our purposes the most important point is that the whole of these ceremonies involve the personification of the tree itself, which cannot be thought of as partaking of apples and cider, except by humane analogy.   This, then, was the first point that we had to establish, namely, that there is evidence of a surviving ritual of the apple-tree, which would almost inevitably result in the projection of the tree into a personal form, just in the same way as the oak-tree inhabited by the lightning becomes the woodpecker and ultimately Zeus himself.   We have not, as yet, supplied evidence to enable us to say whether there was an annual death of the apple-spirit celebrated, nor whether it was a death by violence ; nor can we say whether the image of Christ, which appears to have been carried about by wassailers in Yorkshire, has replaced an earlier image.   Further investigations may throw light on these points.   All that we have proved is the existence of an apple-tree spirit as an object of cult. That is the reply, the first stage of the reply, to those who say that there is no trace of an apple-god in the north of Europe.   Let us see whether we can take further steps to capture this elusive apple-spirit.

CHAPTER II.

THE APPLE-BIRD AND THE APPLE-BOY.

WE may supplement our statements as to the custom of wassailing the apple-trees in Devonshire by extracts from a special report made on the subject by a Committee on Devonshire Folk-Lore, whose report is printed in *Transactions of the Devonshire Association* for 1905 (vol. xxxvii.). The extracts which follow will show how late the custom persisted (it may still be extant for all I know), and will introduce to us the apple-spirit under a new form. Mr. R. H. Jordan of Teignmouth says : " I remember in my younger days (a long time ago) being told of the custom of *firing at the apple-trees on the night of Twelfth Day*, being carried out in several country places in Devonshire ; and I especially remember an old gentleman, who had resided for many years at Bovey Tracey, informing me that when it was done there was a song sung, a part of which I remember :—

> Bear and blow,
> Apples enow,
> Hats full, caps full, bushels full, etc."

In *Devon Notes and Queries*, vol. iii., p. 113, Mr. Henry Gibbon communicates (1) a curious parallel to the cult of the fruit-tree from Japan, (2) a report of the Devonshire custom taken from the Christmas number of the *Illustrated London News* for 1901.

1. Dr. Aston, late British Consul at Seoul, writes : " There is a custom in Japan, in places where there are fruit-trees, for two men to go to the orchard on the last day of the year. *One of the men climbs up a tree*, while the other stands at the bottom, axe in hand. The latter, addressing the tree, asks whether it will bear fruit well or not in the coming year ; otherwise it will be cut down. Then the man up in the tree replies, ' I will bear well '. The effect of this little drama

is said to be very satisfactory." We add an illustration of the Japanese custom from a Carian coin, which appears to have a similar meaning.[1]

PLATE I

2. In this case (the Devonshire custom) the means adopted was bribery, not intimidation. On Christmas Day the owner of the orchard and his people place a cake on the fork of an apple-tree and pour wine on it, while the women chant a chorus, " Bear barns full, sacks full, bags full ".

The Japanese parallel is very interesting, as one of the men employed is put up into the tree to answer for the tree. *For the occasion he is the tree-spirit.* (Parallels not very remote can be found in the Gospels.)[2]

Mr. Gibbon inquired for further details as to the custom, and educed a shoal of references, many of which have been already alluded to.

It is noted that Mrs. Bray in 1832 in her book *Borders of the Tamar and Tavy*, 1879, vol. i., p. 290, was apparently the first to mention " placing bits of toast on the branches ".

" A writer in *Notes and Queries* for 1851 (1st series, iv., p. 309) speaks of a preliminary feasting, at which hot wheat flour cakes were dipped in the cider and eaten : later in the evening a cake was deposited on a fork of the tree and cider thrown over it, etc."

We come next to a very important communication, taken from the *Transactions of the Devon Association*, vol. viii., p. 49. "Miss Pinchard [of Tor, Torquay] in 1876 says that *a little boy was hoisted up into the tree, and seated on a branch. He was to represent a tom-tit*, and sit there crying ' Tit, tit, more to eat ' ; on which some of the bread and cheese and cider was handed up to him."

[1] See British Mus. Coins, Caria, vi., 7.
[2] Professor Elliot Smith draws my attention to a statement in Gubernatis, *Mythologie des Plantes* (i., 5, n. 1) ; " Près de Messine et lorsque le Christ est ressuscité, les paysans qui ont des arbres steriles, vont pour les couper ; un compagnon qui est toujours présent intercède en faveur des arbres qu'on laisse vivre dans l'espoir que le Christ resuscité les a fécondés ".

Mr. A. P. Chope, who draws attention to this feature, makes the parallel with the Japanese custom described above and says acutely that " the boy is evidently the personification of the spirit of the apple-tree, and the libations and offerings are intended to propitiate the spirit in order to obtain a good crop in the coming year. The firing of guns may possibly be intended to frighten away the evil spirits of blight and disease ; but, as this seems to be a recent addition to the custom, its object is more likely to emphasise the shouting."

What the writer did not see was that there was another personification of the tree looking out upon us, just as the woodpecker looks out from the oak-tree over the shoulder of Zeus. This time it is a tom-tit ! The suggestion arises that there was an annual sacrifice of an apple-tree bird, just as there still survives an annual ceremonial slaughter of a woodpecker in the Carpathian mountains. The account in which the boy eats the sacramental bread and drinks the sacramental cider on behalf of the tree is very suggestive. Mr. Chope saw clearly that the firing of guns was late, but here he drifted into rationalism, not suspecting that the guns had replaced earlier weapons of attacking the tree-spirit.

We might note that, if the trees are actually fired at or beaten, whether in their own bodies or in their personifications, it is just as correct to speak of the ritual as intimidation as it is to call it bribery.

Mr. Chope's communication brought out [one from Mr. P. F. S. Amery, showing that the custom was common in the Ashburton district down to the fifties, and continued for some time later. " All the old men spoke of it as having been usual in their younger days. The last occasion in which I took part was on 5 January, 1887, when a party of young men proceeded to our orchard and vigorously saluted the trees with volleys from shotted guns, accompanied by cider drinking, shouting the old charm :—

Here's to thee, old apple tree, etc."

Then follows some more unnecessary rationalism as to the possible good effect of the firing of guns in detaching insects from the bark, etc.

In Devon *Notes and Queries*, vol. iii., p. 156, Mr. H. C. Adams writes that the trees are charmed in different ways at different places. " I never saw it done in Devonshire, but in my early days I lived in Somersetshire, in the parish of Winchcombe, about four miles over the border from Devonshire, and the custom was regularly kept

up there, and I believe it is still, and I have often seen it, and the ceremony was as follows :—

"On the evening (*query*, on the eve) of Twelfth Day a number of
people formed a circle round one of the apple-trees ; some had guns,
some old tin kettles, or any tin tray or other thing that would make a
loud noise when struck with a poker or fire-shovel.   Then the leader
of the party sang a song of which I can only remember one verse :—

> There was an old man,
> And he had an old cow,
> And how to keep her he didn't know how :
> So he built up a barn
> To keep this cow warm,
> And a little more cider would do us no harm.
> Harm, my boys, harm !
> Harm, my boys, harm !
> A little more cider would do us no harm.

The guns were fired and tea-kettles and trays banged, and *then all
stooped down, and raising themselves up three times shouted,*
'*Now, now, now :* hats full, caps full, three bushel bags full, and a
little heap under the stairs ; please God send a good crop,' and then
'Now, now, now,' again, and more gun-firing and kettle-banging, after
which the cider was passed round and another verse was sung with the
same ceremony '."

There are some archaic touches about this.   The people stooping
three times and lifting themselves up, is a bit of sympathetic magic to
represent the lifting and carrying of heavily laden bags of apples.   It
seems to be a part of the primitive ritual, and to be connected with the
three bushel bags in the chant, which we have found elsewhere.

In this account the gun-firing is clearly a case of making as much
noise as possible ; that is shown by the accompaniment, but this idea
need not be regarded as archaic.   The guns may have replaced arrows.

Note.—As Miss Pinchard's communication is so important, I print in a
note the full text as follows :—

"*Blessing of Apple-trees.*   A few years ago, hearing that the ceremony
of ' blessing the apple-trees ' had been celebrated a night or two before in
an orchard close to my house, in the parish of Tormohun, I sent for one of
the party who had been officially engaged in the affair to tell me all particu-
lars concerning it.

"He told me that, after partaking of a good supper provided by the
owner of the orchard, they all, men, women, and children, proceeded to the

orchard, carrying with them a supply of bread, cheese, and cider. They then, all being assembled under one of the best apple-trees, hoisted a little boy up and seated him on a branch. *He, it seems, was to represent a tom-tit,* and sat there crying out : ' Tit, tit ; more to eat ' ; on which some of the bread and cheese and cider was handed up to him. He still *sitting in the tree,* the whole party stood round, each being provided with a little cup, which was forthwith filled with cider, and they then sang the following toast :—

> Here's to thee, good apple-tree,
> To bear and blow, apples enow,
> This year, next year, and the year after too ;
> Hatsful, capsful, three-bushel bagsful,
> And pay the farmer well.

" They then drank all round and fired a salute to the trees, making as much noise as possible with all the pistols, guns, or other old firearms they could collect ; or, failing such, with explosions of gunpowder placed in holes bored in pieces of wood, accompanying the salute with loud cheering and then *firing into the branches of the trees.*
" They then again stood round, and, after another cup of cider, sang :—

> To your wassail, and my wassail,
> And joy be to our jolly wassail ;

which concluded the ceremony. This is done in dead of winter ; and in some cases, buckets of cider with roasted apples floating in them are carried out, and *the apple-trees pelted with the apples ;* but I am not sure whether he said this was done on the occasion of which I write."

Here is one more account which has reached me from an old newspaper cutting, describing the custom of wassailing. It is valuable, because it contains a new method of making the apple-tree drink its own cider. This time, the branches of the tree are actually dipped in the liquid, instead of pouring it out over the root. There is no doubt that the tree drinks. Evidence on that point is cumulative and final.

" Quaint New Year Customs.

" Wassailing the orchard. A New Year custom in the cider counties. After serenading the farmer, the rustics make a ' cheerful noise ' in the orchard, dipping a branch of each apple-tree into a jar of cider, and exhorting them to be fruitful during the coming season.
" It is in the cider-producing counties in the West of England, Devon, Gloucester, Somerset, and Hereford that one of the most picturesque of old-time New Year customs still survives. The ceremony is called ' wassailing the orchard,' and it is supposed to ensure a good crop of apples for the ensuing season. A body of villagers first serenade the

farmer whose apple-trees they have come to bless with a song several verses in length, of which the first is :—

> Wassail, wassail, all over the town,
> The cup is white and the ale is brown :
> Our bowl is made of the good maple-tree,
> And so is the beer of the best of barlie.
> For it's your wassail, and our wassail,
> And jolly come to our merry wassail.

" Having been refreshed, the wassailers proceed to the orchard and surround various chosen trees, making a ' cheerful noise ' with pokers, tongs, and any piece of metal that may be at hand.   There they dip a branch of each tree in a large jar of cider which has been brought for the purpose, and afterwards place a little salt and some crumbs in the angle formed by the tree in the lowest bough.   This ceremony is accompanied by the singing of :—

> Cadbury [1] tree
> I am come to wassail thee,
> To bear and to blow,
> Apples enow,
> Hatfuls, capfuls, and three cornered sackfuls,
> Hollo, boys, Ho !

rendered by the full strength of the company.   This quaint custom is carried out both on New Year's Eve and New Year's Night, and in some districts on Old Twelfth Night also."

The study of the folk-lore of the custom of wassailing the apple-trees has involved frequent repetitions, and some of the writers quoted are not independent of one another.   It was necessary to collect as many references as were accessible, because it often happens in the pursuit of a lost custom of antiquity that one fragment of the rite is found in one place and another fragment in another, so that it is only by a careful collection of the fragments that we can restore the original mosaic, so as to make intelligible history.   For example, in the preceding inquiry, we found little more at the first search than a charm for fertility which appeared in the guise of a communion service, with some traces of violence offered to the tree which was the centre of the rite : and it was not until we unearthed the Torquay custom of sending a boy up into the tree and pretending that the boy was a bird, that we had the parallel personification to the woodpecker as Zeus in the oak-tree.

[1] Query, the charm as performed in the village of Cadbury.

If the object of putting the bird-boy into the tree is the personification of the tree for ritual purposes, it is also clear from what has preceded that the ritual is a charm for fertility : and we are entitled to make parallels with similar cults in other quarters. For example, the practice of the Huzuls in the Carpathian mountains is to ceremonially kill and eat the sacred woodpecker once a year. Is there any trace of a similar sacrifice of the apple-bird ? Did they kill and eat the tom-tit in primitive Devonshire ? As soon as we state the question, we recall to mind the curious custom of killing the wren on St. Stephen's Day, which still prevails in the Isle of Man, in Ireland, in France, and elsewhere. It is a natural supposition that the tom-tit may really be a wren.[1] The custom of killing the wren has been carefully studied by a number of investigators, notably by Sir J. G. Frazer in the second volume of the *Spirits of the Corn and the Wild* (p. 319). We learn that in the Isle of Man on Christmas Eve the wren is hunted and carried in procession with quaint rhymes. " Boys went from door to door with a wren suspended by the legs in the centre of two hoops, which crossed each other at right angles and were decorated with evergreens and ribbons." On St. Stephen's Day, 26 December, the wren was buried, but it is significantly reported that " the bearers say certain lines in which reference is made to boiling and eating the bird ". No doubt this was the earlier form of the rite, before the practice of burying the bird. The coincidence with the woodpecker cult is here very close.

The Irish sing a song over the wren describing him as the *King of all birds* :—

> The wren, the wren, *the King of all birds*,
> St. Stephen's Day was caught in the furze :
> Although he is little his family's great,
> I pray you, good landlady, give us a treat.

Elsewhere in South Wales and in France the ceremonies of King Wren are practised on Twelfth Day, which brings it very close to the wassailing time of the apple-trees. In one district in France the person who finds the wren becomes himself the King, is decorated with mock royalty, and the wren is carried before him " fastened on the top of a pole which is adorned with a verdant wreath of olive, of oak, and

---

[1] The transition is quite easy ; in Norfolk, for instance, the wren is actually known as a tom-tit. Swainson, *Folk-Lore of Birds*, p. 35.

sometimes of *mistletoe grown on an oak* ".   Here we have the second degree of personification which answers to the Devonshire boy who is the tom-tit.

Suppose then we replace the tom-tit by the wren, and agree that the cult involves an actual sacrifice ; can we see any further through the mists of antiquity and into the beliefs of the past ?   Perhaps we can get a step or two further.

It is natural to suspect that if the wren has been replaced by the tom-tit, it has itself replaced the robin : for according to popular tradition the robin is the mate of the wren ; according to the popular rhyme :—

> The robin and the wren
> Are God's cock and hen.[1]

This takes us at once into the region of known thunder-birds, who are sacred on account of their colour symbolism.   There is, however, another reason which can be adduced for the displacement : it will be remembered that what we are studying is a charm for fertility : now in such charms, the female has the right of way against the male : because the woman is the fertile element in humanity, and in that sense agriculture is necessarily of the woman.   That is why the wren replaces the robin : but if this be so, we should expect that the human representative would be not a boy in the tree, but a girl ; or at least, that the sacrificial representative of the tree should be a girl by preference. Apart from this consideration, the tree itself, considered as fruit-bearing, is commonly regarded as feminine, which leads again to a feminine personification.   Do we find any trace of such a choice, or of an alternative custom ?

The evidence which we have so far collected does not help us to answer the question, and the only modern custom that suggests something of the kind is that, in some parts of the south of France, there is a rivalry between the men and women of a district as to which of them shall capture the wren for the Twelfth Day ceremonies.   But if there is no evidence from Devonshire, and no conclusive evidence from France, when we turn to Greek Archæology, we can readily find what we are in search of.

---

[1] The wren is called the King of Birds in the ceremonies for his slaughter, but I am informed that in some parts of the Isle of Man, it is known as the Queen of Birds, which expresses its feminine nature, and connects it, as above, with the robin, as the original King of Birds.

Up to the present point in the discussion, we have not drawn at all on classical parallels, being content to restore from modern practice and tradition the apple-cult with its boy-and-bird personification and sacrifice.   Let us now see if we can find Greek illustrations of charms for fertility involving the placing of a girl in the branches of the tree that is to be fertilised.   If we can find such illustrations they will be a just parallel to our apple-boy.   The tree in question, which we are to search for, need not be an apple-tree, but it should be, one would naturally suppose, a fruit-tree, for otherwise there is no special object in its fertilisation.

Those who are familiar with Greek numismatics know that there is a superb series of Cretan coins, chiefly of the city of Gortyna, which have on one side of them a female figure seated in the branches of a tree, variously described as Europa or Britomartis.   The maiden is visited or at all events accompanied, by a bird, variously recognised as the eagle of Zeus (*i.e.*, Zeus in the form of an eagle), or some much

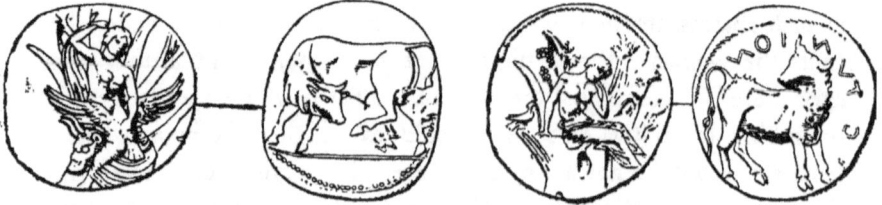

PLATE II   PLATE III

smaller bird (which may be the eagle again, on the hypothesis that Zeus made himself small to avoid scaring the maiden !).   Mr. A. B. Cook points out, by setting some of these coins in series, that the conjunction of the bird and the maiden is accompanied by a bursting into life and leaf of the tree.[1]   Here are two of such coins, one from the British Museum (Crete, Pl. X. 5), the other from the Maclean Collection.

All that I am concerned with at this point, is that the presence of the girl in the tree accompanied by the bird is a charm for fertility, and that we have before us the exact parallel to the Devonshire boy and the tom-tit : or if it is not quite exact, the variation, may, perhaps, lie

---

[1] He thinks it is a pollard willow, which is something like transplanting Cambridge into Crete.   According to Theophrastus it was a plane-tree, a statement which appears to have had wide currency.

in the fact that the boy is sacrificed, and the girl, perhaps, ceremonially married.   The end in either case is the same, the securing of the next year's crop or harvest.

Now let us go a little further and see if we can find the boy in the tree as well as the girl.

Among the coins of Phaestos in Crete we find representations of a god, or at least a tree-spirit equivalent to a god, seated in a tree and holding in his hand a cock.   The figure is commonly described as Zeus Felcanos, the latter name being inscribed across the coin.[1]   Here, then,

PLATE IV

we have the same conjunction of bird-form and human-form with the tree-form.   The tree is evidently the same leafless tree as in the Gortyna coins ; like these coins too (it is a point to be noted), the tree has a strongly defined hollow, which may be an original woodpecker-hole. In any case, the tree is hollow.

Comparing the Phaestos coins with those of Gortyna, we see that in each case we have a tree-spirit posing for fertility in the branches under the twofold representation of bird and human being.   The Phaestos-figure is called Zeus, on the faith of a gloss of Hesychius that Felcanos is a name of Zeus among the Cretans.   It is a very young Zeus, if it is Zeus, and certainly not the father of gods and men. Svoronos describes him as follows :—

" Zeus Felchanos *représenté comme jeune homme nu*, assis à gauche sur un arbre, posant la main droite sur un coq, débout à gauche sur ses genoux, s'appuyant de la gauche sur l'arbre."

The boy-Zeus, as I may now call him, is the proper Greek parallel to the Devonshire lad who is both tree and tom-tit.   If there had been any coins of Torquay, they would have shown the same kind of features as we find in the coins of Gortyna and Phaestos.[2]

[1] We give a reproduction of the British Museum Coin (Crete, Pl. XV, 10).

[2] The reference which was made above to the hollow in the tree is important, for the hollow is clearly conventional and stands for something.   In

As a result of our investigations we are now entitled to restore the ritual of the killing of the wren to connection with the ritual of the wassailing of the apple-tree. They are parts of the same ceremony. The wren is missing in the Devonshire ceremony, because the bird has been replaced by a boy (or perhaps a girl). The crossed hoops, however, in which the body of the wren is suspended, we have seen to be a part of the ritual of wassailing among the Wiltshire rustics ; and a cow-horn which is blown by a lad in the Sussex orchards was an especial feature of the ceremony of killing the wren in Manxland.[1]

The parallelism between the apple-cults, the oak-cult, and the cult of the corn-field, is now seen to be very close. In each case we have charms for fertility, addressed to the spirit (corn-spirit, tree-spirit) that is involved.

Thus we have a series of personifications :—

Oak-tree or Thunder.
Woodpecker or Thunder-bird (probably killed and eaten at an annual ceremony).
Zeus or Thunder-god (perhaps preceded by an intermediate stage of oak-boy or oak-girl. The latter, perhaps, the Cretan Europa.)

For the corn-field, we have the corn-spirit as

Last sheaf in the field
Corn-dolly or corn-animal (wolf, cat, pig, man) sacrificed and sometimes eaten.
Corn-mother or Corn-maid. (Demēter and Persephonē.)

For the apple-cult, which is clearly related to the oak-cult, we have

Apple-tree (containing Sky-god through mistletoe).
Apple-bird (Robin, Wren, Tom-tit), probably killed and eaten at an annual ceremony.
Apple-boy or Apple-girl.
Apple-god (Apollo, Balder, or some similar identification).

It has been suggested above that the *killing of the wren* was really a preliminary to the *eating of the wren ;* that is, that the bird

its later forms an incuse square with a well-defined central spot. Apparently this central spot once stood for the head of a bird : see plate AR 23 of Svoronos.
[1] Britton, *Beauties of Wilts,* 1825 : " The custom of wassailing is still continued. A party of men assemble in the evening, and having obtained a cheese-bowl, decorate it with two intersecting hoops, covered with ribands, etc." In Train's *History of the Isle of Man,* we are told that in 1842 no less than four sets of boys engaged in hunting the wren were observed in the town of Douglas, *each party blowing a horn.*

was eaten sacramentally as the representative of the tree-spirit. In Manxland the wren is buried, but the song which is sung over it is in evidence for another kind of sepulchre. This song is given as follows in Train's *History of the Isle of Man* (vol. ii., p. 141, 1845) :—

THE HUNTING OF THE WREN.

We'll away to the woods, says Robin the Bobbin :
We'll away to the woods, says Richard the Robbin.
We'll away to the woods, says Jackey the Land :
We'll away to the woods, says every one.
What will we do there ? says Robin the Bobbin,
                              Repeat as before.
We'll hunt the wren, says, etc.
Where is he, where is he ? says, etc.
In yonder green bush, says, etc.
How can we get him down, says, etc.
With sticks and with stones, says, etc.
He's down, he's down, says, etc.
How can we get him home ? says, etc.
We'll hire a cart, says, etc.
Whose cart shall we hire ? says, etc.
Johnny Bil Fel's says, etc.
How can we get him in, says, etc.
With iron bars, says, etc.
He's at home, he's at home, says, etc.
How will we get him boiled ? says, etc.
In the brewery pan, says, etc.
How will we get him eaten ? says, etc.
With knives and with forks, says, etc.
Who's to dine at the feast ? says, etc.
The king and the queen, says, etc.
The pluck for the poor, says, etc.
The legs for the lame, says, etc.
The bones for the dogs, says, etc.
He's eaten, he's eaten, says, etc.

The music of the wren-song is given in Barrow's *Mona Melodies*, 1820.

For our present purpose, the important point is the survival in the song of the tradition that the wren should be eaten as well as killed. It is as well to record the existence of a musical element in the ceremony, over and above the noise of the cow-horn.

CHAPTER III.

Personification of the Apple-tree (*Continued*).

We may perhaps infer from the occurrence of the two different ways of disposing of the bird, which are suggested by Manx Folklore, that the burying of the wren has replaced the eating of the wren. Folk-songs appear to be in evidence for both forms of the cult.

For, example, there is a song, which is still sung by children in the East End of London, which tells of an old woman who killed a robin, and then planted an apple-tree over its grave. This may very well be another way of saying that the robin as apple-bird was buried at the roots of the apple-tree.[1]

---

[1] The song, as far as I can gather, is to the following effect :—

> Old Robin is dead and gone to his grave,
> Hum ! Ha ! gone to his grave,
> They planted an apple-tree over his head,
> Hum ! Ha ! over his head.
>
> The apples were ripe and ready to drop,
> Hum ! Ha ! ready to drop.
> There came an old woman a-picking them up,
> Hum ! Ha ! picking them up.
>
> Old Robin got up and gave her a knock,
> Hum ! Ha ! gave her a knock,
> Which made the old woman go hipperty-hop,
> Hum ! Ha ! hipperty-hop.

It will interest the people of the North Country to know that the Robin who is buried and comes to life again in the folk-songs of the East End of London, is represented on the coat of arms of the City and the University of Glasgow. Look, for example, at the University shield, which is supposed to represent the miraculous deeds and virtues of St. Kentigern *alias* St. Mungo the early British saint. We have no space to show that St. Mungo is one of the great and glorious company of Twin Saints, but a glance at the shield will show the thunder-bird, as robin, perched on the top of the thunder-tree (in

We ought not to ignore another feature which is suggested by the Manx song, *viz.:* the presence of the King and the Queen, who are to eat the bird. This is evidence not merely for the eating of the apple-bird, but also for the participation in the ceremony of a Twelfth-Night King and Queen, whose ceremonial union is an added charm for fertility. Some such charm was almost inevitable, if sympathetic magic is to have its proper place in the ceremony. In the Isle of Man there is evidence enough that Twelfth Night Eve is a time of general license, which may easily have been religious in the first instance, and perhaps confined to a single pair, who, like Zeus and Europa, represented the union of the sky-god and the tree-spirit. Here is an account from Waldron's *Isle of Man* (A.D. 1731 : Manx. Soc. reprint, 1865, p. 49) :—

"Christmas is ushered in with a form much less meaning and infinitely more fatiguing (than the May-day festival). On 24 December, towards evening, all the servants in general have a holiday, they go not to bed all night, but ramble about till the bells ring in all the Churches, which is at 12 o'clock : prayers being over, they go to hunt the wren, and having found one of these poor birds they kill her, and lay her on a bier with the utmost solemnity, bringing her to the Parish Church, and burying her with a whimsical kind of solemnity, singing dirges over her in the Manx language, which they call her knell, after which Christmas begins. There is not a barn unoccupied the whole twelve days, every parish hiring fiddlers at the public charge ; and all the youth, nay, sometimes people well advanced in years, making no scruple to be among the nocturnal dancers. At this time, there never fails some work being made for Kirk Jarmyns (the St. German's prison) ; so many young fellows and girls meeting in these diversions, etc. etc."

As we have said, the license of the youth in the eighteenth century A.D., is not exactly parallel to that which prevailed in the eighteenth century B.C., when religion, as well as passion, prompted the expression

this case, the oak) ; and when we turn to the legends of St. Kentigern, we shall find that the robin had been killed, and miraculously raised to life again by the saint. In the *Aberdeen Breviary* it is described as *quaedam avicula quae rubesca* (sc. *rubecula*) *dicitur*. Thus the raising to life of the robin is a companion legend to the hunting of the wren. There is much more to be said on the folk-lore of the Glasgow seal and the University coat of arms.

of life in acts that might affect the prosperity of the whole of the ensuing year.   It would be a mistake to think of primitive people as vastly
more wicked than ourselves, and as belonging to a time when there
" aren't no ten commandments " : if there was no decalogue, there was a
myriologue of taboos which preceded the ten.   After all, the ten commandments are a mere abbreviation of supposed duties.

If we are right in regarding the Devonshire boy up the apple-tree
as a fertility demon parallel to the Cretan Europa or Felcanos, the
apple-boy being the key to the understanding of the Cretan oak-boy
and oak-girl, we may now take a further step with the assistance of the
Cretan coinage.   We have examined the coins of Gortyna and of
Phaestos, and have seen the way in which these cities have represented
the tree-spirit, girl or boy as the case may be.   There is another city
in Crete not yet identified, which struck a similar series of coins, *the
place of the tree-spirit being now occupied by Apollo himself.*
The coin to which we draw attention is in the Hunter Collection at
Glasgow, and is figured in Percy Gardner's *Types of Greek Coins,*
Pl. IX, Nos. 15 and 16.   The following is the description in
G. Macdonald, *Catalogue of Greek Coins in the Hunterian
Collection,* Glasgow, 1901, ii., 200, Pl. XLIII, 7.

PLATE V

Uncertain (Town) of Crete.
Silver.   *Fourth Century* B.C.
Æginetic standard
Stater.

Obverse.	Reverse
Male figure, naked to waist, seated r. amid branches of a tree ; he supports himself with r., while he holds large wreath in extended l.	Apollo, seated r. head facing, amid the branches of a laurel ; he holds lyre in l., and plektron in r.

If we assume that the tree on the obverse is identified with the tree
on the reverse, and that the god in the tree is the same on both sides,

then we have to call the god Apollo, and the tree a bay-tree.   Analogy
with the coins of Gortyna and Phaestos suggests that he is in the tree
as a part of a cult for fertility.   The difficult point is to determine what
possible object there could be in fertilising a bay-tree.   Has the bay-
tree displaced some earlier form ?   There is much to favour this belief : we have shown in the Lecture on Apollo in the book called
The Ascent of Olympus, that at Delphi, where Apollo has his own
way with regard to trees and the like, the laurel was not primitive, for,
as Ovid pointed out in describing the fight of Apollo with the python,

nondum laurus erat :

and Apollo found his victor's wreath in a neighbouring oak.   This
should be the very wreath which he is holding on one side of the coin.

We are now very near to finding Apollo as an oak-boy, of the
type of Zeus Felcanos.   The next step from the oak to the apple-tree,
is a missing link in numismatic identification.   We can find coins re-
presenting the god holding the apple, and we can find the sacred
apple-tree at Delphi, but the evidence lacks completeness, and we must
leave the case in the following form : Apollo in Crete in the fourth
century B.C., was a tree-boy, the tree being a bay-tree, with a possible
earlier form, not yet identified.[1]   Now let us leave a blank at this
point for further evidence, if such should be forthcoming, and let us
return to the Isle of Man.

The next thing we come across in the Manx ceremony is a combination of music and mantic, in the person of the fiddler who directs
the dance.   He proceeds to tell the fortune of the coming year to the
young men and maidens assembled.   This is described as follows by
Waldron :—

"On Twelfth Day the fiddler lays his head in some one of the
wenches' laps, and a third person asks who such a maid, or such a
maid, shall marry, naming the girls there present one after another ; to
which he answers according to his own whim, or agreeable to the
intimacies he has taken note of during the time of merriment.   But
whatever he says is as absolutely depended on as an oracle ;
and if he happens to couple two people who have an aversion to each
other, tears and vexation succeed the mirth.   This they call *cutting off*

---

[1] There is some evidence that at Olympia also the primitive prize was
an apple.

the fiddler's head, for after this, he is dead for the whole year. This custom still continues in every parish."

The foregoing account is very striking, it is almost unbelievable that the ill-assorted unions suggested by the fiddler should have oracular force. What force they possess has certainly come down out of the past, and the fiddler must have religious sanction and be a religious figure. The oracle appears as the *Luck of the Year ;* it is congruous with the charms that determine fertility for the fruit-tree. The fiddler is a primitive Apollo, with a fiddle in place of a lyre, not a wide variation in music ; and the suggestion arises that Apollo was originally oracular at a particular time of the year, and that at other times he was quiescent. The girl in whose lap the fiddler lays his head is the prototype of the Pythian priestess who gives the responses for the god.

Those who have read the study of Apollo in the *Ascent of Olympus* will recall the place which the apple takes in Greek Folk-lore ; in this connection, the story of Hermochares and Ktesulla which is there quoted, is very edifying. The apple which Hermochares throws to the dancing maiden has an oracle inscribed on it to the effect that " Ktesulla will marry an Athenian named Hermochares ". This is just the sort of thing which the Manx fiddler would have said upon occasion. It is a reply to the question, " Whom will Ktesulla marry ? " Alas that such an interesting custom should have disappeared !

> Apollo from his shrine
> Can no more divine.

We have to get our answers in another way. The girls give the responses themselves : they have oracular force,

> For if she will, she will, you may depend on't,
> And if she won't, she won't, and there's the end on't.[1]

Traces of the same practice of divination may be noted at the Lenten fires in the district of the Ardennes, and elsewhere. Frazer has described these fires, kindled on the first Sunday in Lent, in *Balder the Beautiful* (i., 109). Here is a striking passage :—

---

[1] The oracular element survives in the old-fashioned game of " forfeits " at Christmas time, when a person is blindfolded, or hides his head in some one's lap, as a preliminary to guessing the answers of certain questions. One type is, Here is a thing, a very pretty thing, and who is the owner of this pretty thing ? " The punishments for wrong answers have often an oracular ambiguity about them, such as " Bite an inch off the poker ".

" At Épinal in the Vosges, on the first Sunday in Lent, bonfires used to be kindled at various places both in the town and on the banks of the Moselle. They consisted of pyramids of sticks and faggots, which had been collected some days earlier by many folks going from door to door. When the flames blazed up, the names of various couples, whether young or old, handsome or ugly, rich or poor, were called out, and the persons thus linked in mock marriage *were forced, whether they liked it or not,* to march arm in arm round the fire amid the laughter and jests of the crowd. The festivity lasted till the fire died out, and then the spectators dispersed through the streets, stopping under the windows of the houses and proclaiming the names of the *féchenots* and *féchenottes* or valentines whom the popular voice had assigned to each other. These couples had to exchange presents : the mock bridegroom gave his mock bride something for her toilet, while she in turn presented him with a cockade of coloured ribbon."

The foregoing account is parallel in many ways to the Twelfth Night divination in the Isle of Man, but the ceremonies are not so serious, and the oracular force is much diminished. The same thing is true of the Hallowe'en divinations, of which we have the following statement in Frazer :—[1]

" In the Highlands of Scotland, as the evening of Hallowe'en wore on, young people gathered in one of the houses and resorted to an almost endless variety of games, or rather, *forms of divination,* for the purpose of ascertaining the future fate of each member of the company. Were they to marry or to remain single, was the marriage to take place this year or never, who was to be married first, what sort of husband or wife he or she was to get, the name, the trade, the colour of the hair, the amount of property of the future spouse—these were questions that were eagerly canvassed and the answers to them furnished never failing entertainment."

Here also there seems to be a lack of seriousness which can hardly be primitive.

[1] *Op. cit.,* i., 234.

CHAPTER IV.

GANYMEDES AND HEBE.

WE have shown that the Devonshire custom of placing a boy in the branches of an apple-tree as a representative of the tree, and as a substitute for a previous bird-representative, is strictly parallel to the development of the oak-cults and thunder-cults, which we were able to trace in Crete and elsewhere. We are now going to show that our investigation is capable of throwing some further light on the problems of Greek mythology.

Returning for the moment to the Torquay custom, we see that the apple-sacrament by which the rustics share with the tree the life of the tree, has developed a human representative, who stands for the tree on the one hand, and for the agriculturist on the other, who is operating with sympathetic magic on the tree. This representative acts as an intermediary, and makes the communion of the tree-spirit and the people into a visible act ; he eats and drinks the products of the tree with the people on the one hand, and with the tree on the other. The cup of cider which is handed to him is a communion cup and a libation vessel. He will give what he gets, in part at least, to the tree.

Since the boy is, admittedly, a bird one degree removed, it is evident that if the bird were to be in the tree at the same time as the boy, then the bird would itself have to be fed in order to make the circle of communion complete.

When we turn from the apple-tree to the oak-tree, we naturally ask what has become of the meal in which the participation of the worshipper and his cult object is accomplished. Does the oak-tree also eat and drink, or does any bird or boy eat and drink with it ?

This brings to our mind one of the perplexing features of the Greek mythology, of which no satisfactory explanation has ever been offered : the presence of a pair of cup-bearers, male and female, among the Olympian gods, named respectively Ganymedes and Hebe. They

PLATE VII.—FROM CARL ROBERT: "DIE ANTIKEN SARKOPHAG-RELIEFS," VOL. II, PLATE 2, FIG. 4

are evidently closely related, for Hebe has sometimes the title of Ganymeda, and she stands in relation to Hera, much in the same light as Ganymedes to Zeus. Each of them is a cup-bearer of the gods.

Now in Greek art, it is easy to see that Ganymedes has been cup-bearer to the eagle that carried him off, before he has himself become an adjunct of Olympus. We constantly find him represented as presenting the bowl of nectar to the eagle ; certainly the eagle stands for Zeus in this connection, but it is Zeus in disguise, and away from Olympus.[1] Ganymedes is really giving drink to the thunder-bird, who precedes the thunder-man, and the thunder-bird is the oak-bird.

PLATE VI

We can see this expressed in many ways by the Greek artists, who will place an oak-tree in the field of view, near to Ganymedes, or in a position where he can lean up against it. Sometimes the oak is further specified by the depicting of acorns upon it, and sometimes *Ganymedes is actually giving the eagle to drink out of an acorn-cup.* We see, then, clearly that Ganymedes is the oak-tree boy ; he represents the spirit of the tree, whom he propitiates through the bird by the food and drink which he has with him, exactly as the Devonshire apple-boy does. This was the way in which he became cup-bearer to Zeus ; he was cup-bearer to the thunder-tree and to the thunder-bird ; to the oak-tree and to the oak-bird.[2] Thus he is something like Dionysos in being a visible Zeus, a palpable, though diminished, King of the Wood ; and it is as such a little Zeus, that upon one of the earliest Greek vases, we find him crowned by Hera, Zeus looking on, and Hebe, his female counterpart, standing behind

[1] The gem which is here represented will be found in Furtwängler, Pl. LXV, 52.

[2] The accompanying plate (Robert. vol. ii., Pl. II, Fig. 4) shows the eagle twice over, and the oak-tree also in duplicate ; the acorn-cup should also be noted.

Hera : the cock, as thunder-bird, is in the picture instead of the eagle, just as he appears on the Felcanos coins of Phaestos.[1] The only direction in which there is a want of parallel, is that Ganymedes does not actually sit in the branches of a tree, as do Europa and Zeus Felcanos. This is not a very important omission in view of the fact that the tree is so often in the representation. We take it, then, that Ganymedes and the eagle are practising an annual charm for fertilisation of the oak-tree, and that what is represented on the coins and gems which we have been describing is a religious ceremony : we have given back Greek art to Greek religion, and restored Ganymedes to respectability.

This is not all that we learn from our apple-cult in its Devonshire and other related forms. It will be remembered that we found out that food and drink were given to the tree, or to the representatives of the tree, from the products of the tree itself. The tree is medicined from the food and drink which its own nature supplies, apples and cider being the food and drink in question. When we come to the case of the oak-tree, we see that the eagle is actually being supplied with drink, but what is the drink in question ? Evidently it is the same drink that is supplied to the Olympians, the nectar of the gods, which answers very closely to the Soma that is offered to the Vedic deities. How can this drink be in any way connected with the oak-tree, or indeed any drink, for we can hardly suppose that a brew was made of acorns. There are only two directions in which I see any possibility of solving the riddle. The drink must be made out of the sacred honey, which leads at once to the identification of nectar with some form of intoxicating mead (cf. μέθυ and μεθύω) ; or else it is a drink prepared from the ivy, ivy being considered as a part of the oak-tree, and related to it as Dionysos to Zeus.

It is not impossible that the two points of view may have been combined, just as in the ivy-ale at Ascension-tide in Lincoln College, Oxford. The nectar can hardly have been fermented ivy-juice, pure

---

[1] Hackl says of the Munich vase that Hera (?) holds a crown over the head of Ganymedes. If that be correct it is perhaps a crown of oak-leaves, and Ganymedes is the King of the Wood. Mr. A. B. Cook objects that " a black-figured vase of this early date would certainly represent a wreath as a black circle ". He thinks that Hera is holding a plate of apples or more probably pomegranates over Ganymedes' head.

PLATE VIII.—FROM SEYERING AND HACKL: "DIE KOENIGLICHE VASENSAMMLUNG ZU MÜNCHEN," PAGE 95, FIG. 94

and simple ; yet it can hardly have been without the presence of ivy : for Hebe who administers it, appears to have worn an ivy-crown at her cult centres, and at Phlios in particular, which is her chief place of worship, there was an annual ceremony of ivy-cutting, which must surely be related to the Cult of Hebe herself.

Thus the suggestion arises that in the composition of the original Soma-drink, which makes and maintains the immortality of the Aryan gods, ivy had a prominent place. Its combination with honey-mead will explain all the references which have hitherto been brought forward to prove that Soma was a honey-drink. We know from the Vedas that it was, primarily, the juice of a plant. The plant was the ivy.

From the description in the Vedas, it is easy to infer that Soma was a plant, a mountain plant, with long tendrils ; that it grew on the rocks and apparently also on trees ; that it was crushed between stones, strained through a wool-strainer, was yellow in colour (which may refer either to the juice or to the berries of the plant, and would answer very well to some kinds of ivy), and that it became an intoxicant and was as such personified and took its place by Indra in the Vedic pantheon.

For the supposition that the Soma-drink was composite in character, we may refer to Macdonell, *Vedic Mythology*, who remarks that Soma was mixed with mead : that the term " *madhu* . . . is especially applied to the Soma-juice " (p. 105) : that " the juice is *honied* (*madhumat*). The latter expression seems to have meant ' sweetened with honey,' *some passages pointing to the admixture*." He sums up the Soma question as follows : " The belief in an intoxicating divine beverage, the home of which was heaven, may be Indo-European. If so, it must have been regarded as a kind of honey-mead, brought down to earth from its guardian demon by an eagle, the Soma-bringing eagle of Indra agreeing with the nectar-bringing eagle of Zeus, and with the eagle which as a metamorphosis of Odhin carried off the mead. This Madhu, or honey-mead, if Indo-European, was replaced in the Indo-Iranian period by Soma ; but may have survived into the Vedic period *by amalgamating with Soma*" (p. 114).

" Amalgamation with Soma " is another way of saying that the juice of the Soma plant was sweetened with honey, in some fermented form.

The equation between Soma and nectar appears to be established ; the philological interpretations are more obscure. The latest explanation of *nectar* explains it in terms of the immortality which it confers, as a " death-destroyer, from the two roots νεκ (as in νέκυς, νεκρός, Lat. *necem*), and a stem which underlies the Greek τείρω ' to rub,' ' to wear out ' ".[1]

It stands, therefore, not for the products out of which it is made (honey, ivy, or both), but for the intoxicating quality which it possesses. For the Devonshire wassailers I suppose that cider would be a just equivalent of Soma.

Another title of Soma is " amṛta," which conveys exactly the sense and very nearly the form of the Greek ἄμβροτυς. Philologically, then, we are entitled to equate Soma with nectar.

---

[1] See Boisacq, *Dict. Étym. de la langue Grecque* (Paris, 1913), follow-ing closely on the track of Prellwitz, *Étym. Wört. d. Griech. Sprache* (Göttingen, 1915), equates the meaning of "nectar" with that of " Am-brosia ".

CHAPTER V.

The Name of the Apple-God.

We have shown that there was a tendency towards personification in the ritual of the apple-orchard ; it was, indeed, difficult to resist such a tendency when one had to ask questions of a tree as to its future conduct, or when one had to share with a tree its life-blood, and apply that life-blood to the life of the tree itself. We pointed out that in the case of the apple-tree, the personification was in the first place through a bird (male or female) that was a denizen of the tree, and, in the next case, through a boy or girl substituted for the bird, or thought of in connection with it. Amongst such tree-boys and tree-girls for representatives of oak, apple, and laurel we were able to recognise by name

> Europa, or, according to some,
> Britomartis.
> Ganymedes and Hebe, and
> Apollo.

The first three were oak-boys and oak-girls ; the last appeared as a laurel-boy or bay-boy, with a probability that an oak-boy or apple-boy was behind the form which we discovered. The Cretan evidence was admitted to be incomplete, but it was important as far as it went. It certainly disclosed Apollo as a tree-boy, in a form not unlike the Devonshire apple-boy. Returning now to the north of Europe, we take up the inquiry as to the meaning of the Balder legend. The story of Balder the Beautiful and of his tragic death by an arrow of mistletoe is well known. He was the darling of the northern gods, and of the goddess Frigg in particular. She, Frigg, " took an oath from fire and water, iron and all metals, stones and earth, and from trees, sicknesses, and from poisons, and from all four-footed beasts, birds, and creeping things, that they would not hurt Balder. When this was done, Balder was deemed invulnerable : so the gods amused

43

themselves by setting him in their midst, while some shot at him, others hewed at him, and others threw stones at him." [1]

But Frigg had forgotten to include the mistletoe among the possible enemies of Balder : so had not the malicious Loki, who fashioned an arrow out of mistletoe, and showed the blind god Holdr how to aim it at Balder. So Balder died by the mistletoe, and there was much wailing of gods and goddesses on his account.

Upon the whole story Frazer remarks that "whatever may be thought of an historical kernel underlying a mythical husk in the legend of Balder, the details of the story suggest that it belongs to a class of myths which have been dramatised in ritual, or to put it otherwise, which have been performed as magical ceremonies for the sake of producing those natural effects which they describe in figurative language". [2]

Frazer thinks that Balder is the personification of a mistletoe-bearing oak, and that he was burned at midsummer, perhaps in the form of an actual sacrifice.

We suggest that the mistletoe-bearing oak be changed to a mistletoe-bearing apple-tree, and that midwinter be substituted for midsummer as the time of the sacrifice of the tree-boy. The curse of Frigg will then be a description of the spells which are said over the apple-tree in some such form as the following :—

> No fire touch thee :
> No water drown thee :
> No iron come near thee :
> No blight affect thee :
> No beast beset thee :
> Good apple-tree.

The gods will then represent the rustics attacking the tree with sticks and stones which are not meant to hurt it, and attacking the apple-bird or apple-boy with sticks and stones that are meant to hurt, so that the life of the personified tree may be given for the annual reinforcement of the tree itself.

Another reason why we say that Balder is the Northern Apollo and the personified apple-tree is that his name invited the supposition. We have shown (in the Rylands Library Lecture on " Apollo ") that the word " apple," in its primitive form " abàl," had the accent on the

---

[1] Frazer, *Balder the Beautiful*, i., 101.
[2] *Ibid.*, i., 105.

second syllable ; when suffixes were attached to the word, the forward accent released the initial vowel, and left the syllable " bal ".

Now the name for " apple-tree " is found in early charters as a place-name in the form " Appledore," " Apuldre," closely related to which are the forms *Apfalter, Affalter, Affolter*, in the Middle High Dutch.   Upon these names I remarked as follows in the Rylands Lecture on the " Cult of Artemis ":—[1]

" It has occurred to me that perhaps the ' apel-dur,' ' apel-dre,' and ' appeldore,' which we have been considering may be the origin of Balder (and of Paltar of Grimm's hypothesis), in view of the occurrence of the corresponding forms mentioned above in the Middle High Dutch. If, for instance, the original accent in *apple* (abãl) is, as stated above, on the second syllable, then it would be easy for a primitive *apál-dur* to lose its initial vowel, and in that case we should not be very far from the form *Balder*, which would mean the apple-tree originally and nothing more."

According to these suggestions Balder is the apple-boy, because Balder is apple-tree.   It is interesting to see whether the beautiful Northern god has left his mark on the place-names or personal names in this country.   For instance, there is a personal name Baldrewood (an English novelist) and another Balderston, but these are clearly place-names used to denote persons.   Balderwood, for instance, occurs in the New Forest.   On the other hand, Balderson appears to be a real personal name, corresponding to the Greek Apollonides.   In Yorkshire we have Baldersby as a place-name, certainly Scandinavian, and in Lancashire, Balderstone.   The Greek parallel would be Apollonia. In Cheshire and Notts we have Balderton.   There is another near Wrexham in North Wales.   I do not know any Balders or Bolders in the Midlands.

It is possible that the arrow-struck apple-tree spirit has been perpetuated in the Christian St. Sebastian, whose festival is a fortnight later than Twelfth Day (Epiphany), and whose death is due, (i) to a shower of arrows, (ii) to beating with clubs.

But this requires closer examination.   Was not the tomb of Sebastian found in the Catacomb of St. Calixtus ?

It will be asked whether, if we are correct in interpreting Balder as the apple-tree, and the oath taken by Frigg as the spells for the good

[1] P. 64.

luck of the apple-tree, and the beating of Balder with sticks and stones.
as a part of the rustic ritual, we ought to omit the pathetic part of the
Balder story, where his wife Nanna insists on accompanying him to
the lower world. According to the Edda, when Balder's body was
placed upon the funeral pile upon his ship, his wife Nanna saw it, died
of grief, and was laid on the same funeral pile as her husband.

It is not an unnatural question as to whether Nanna is merely a
lay-figure in the mythology, or whether she also has to be interpreted.
The only directions in which an interpretation seems possible are (1)
that the sacrifice of Balder the tree-boy has been accompanied not only
by a mystical marriage with the view of fertility, but by a sacrifice of
the tree-girl as well as the tree-boy ; (2) that a pair of trees might
have been associated together, and thought of as married, in which
case the rites for fertilising the first would naturally apply to the second.
The two points of view suggested are not necessarily exclusive.

The marriage of trees is still practised in India : let us see what is
said on this curious custom.

" The *aswatta* (or *pipal*) tree is consecrated to Vishnu, or rather
it is *Vishnu himself under the form of a tree*. . . . Sometimes it
is solemnly married. Generally a *vepu* or margosa tree is selected for
its spouse, and occasionally a plantain or banana tree. Almost the
same formalities are observed for this curious marriage as in the case of
a marriage between Brahmins. Here and there on the high roads and
elsewhere the *aswatta* and *vepu* trees may be seen planted side by
side on little mounds. This union is not an accidental one, but the
result of an actual marriage ceremony. Not thirty yards from the
modest hut where these pages were written were two of these trees,
under whose shade I have often reclined. Their trunks were so closely
entwined that they had become incorporated one with another. The
inhabitants of the village could remember to have seen them planted
together some fifty years before, and said that they had been present
at the wedding festivities, which lasted several days, and were celebrated at the expense of a wealthy person of the neighbourhood at a
cost of more than 1500 rupees." [1]

There is, then, nothing impossible in the idea of an actual tree-
marriage. The explanation of this quaint belief may lie in various

[1] Dubois and Beauchamp, *Hindu Manners, Customs, and Ceremonies*
(3rd ed., p. 653).

directions ; it would be quite natural in the case of a pair of trees of the same species, one of which was male and the other female (as the wild fig-tree and the fruit-bearing fig-tree) : but how are we to explain the union where the trees are diverse ? The suggestion arises that it may be due to the use of a pair of fire-sticks, male and female, which might be made from the same tree, or, as was often the case, from two different trees, a hard-wood male tree and a relatively softer female tree. In some such way, then, the idea of the tree-marriage might have been arrived at. The Hindu practice certainly assists the imagination in finding a place for Nanna the Faithful by the side of Balder the Beautiful. It also helps us, by its identification of the *aswatta* tree with Vishnu, to understand better the personifications of the tree-spirit which we have come across in Western folk-lore and mythology.

APPENDIX.

SINCE writing the preceding essay I have received the following interesting communication from a South Devonian who has actually "wassailed" the apple-trees—Mr. P. G. Bond, of Plymouth (a member of the *Plymouth Institution*),—who also reminds me of the prevalence in his youthful days of the custom of cutting the "neck" of the harvest; of this corn-ritual there is much more surviving evidence than for the "wassailing" of the apples. His reminiscence may very well be added to the general folk-lore tradition.

WASSAILING THE APPLE-TREE.

BY P. G. BOND, M.R.C.V.S., PLYMOUTH.

What was no doubt the last flickering remains of this local custom confined to the cider district of the South Hams, in the County of Devon, came under my notice in or about the year 1860, fifty-eight years ago.

I may be said to have taken part in it, although I did not know anything about the custom, its origin, its significance, or its mode of procedure. At the time I was eight years old. The scene was either at an old farm called Henacres Farm, an off-farm of Rack Park Farm in the occupation of my aunt, near Washbrook Mill in the parish of Dodbrooke, or at the mill. I had as schoolfellow a son of the miller, Stephen Cole.

I very frequently spent the Saturday at the mill with him and his family, returning home about 4 o'clock in the afternoon.

The mill apple orchard adjoined the mill; it was entered by a gate from the main road, and also by a gate from the mill yard. The best apple-tree stood about 12 to 15 feet in from the roadway gate. Another apple orchard was in connection with Henacres Farm, and the best and most prolific tree on it was one bearing the apple called the "Royal Red Streak".

On this occasion it was Christmas Eve not Twelfth Eve, of that I am not in doubt. On Christmas Eve there would be usually a good many callers, customers of the miller, and friends of the house ; they called to give the compliments of the season and receive them. The drink offered was warmed cider in which were placed baked apples. The cake offered was a good currant cake, there was no deficiency of fruit. The health of the household was drunk, and the health of the apple-trees.

Words said to have been used :—

" Here's a health to the good apple-tree, may we all have cap fulls, pocket fulls, sack fulls," or words to that effect.

I do not remember them myself ; the cider cup was passed around to all and sundry with the cake. I do not remember any gun being fired off at the tree ; this was a Somersetshire custom, not usually done in Devon. The wassailing died out and did not maintain its hold as did the " crying of the neck ".

In a note I made some years ago, I find as follows :—

" I heard the Knack cried in 1865 at Dudbrooke Hills on Cranch's ground, part of Aunt Bond's farm, it was cried by a man called William Hodge who repeated the following words :—

" ' We've ploughed and we've sowed, we've reaped and we've mowed. Neck.' " This was said three times, and those looking on walked slowly round a sheaf of corn. The knack was called over the last sheaf of wheat cut on the farm for that harvest.

William Hodge was foreman and horsekeeper at Rack Park Farm, the Home Farm, and at Dodbrooke Henacres Farm.

Cranch's ground where the " neck" was cried was an off-part of the farm. Hodge was the arch priest of the folk-lore.

In looking back so long to pick up the memory of the past, I begin to think I heard more of this old custom and wassailing than I saw of it. I have not any note in connection with it, so I am uncertain. I have heard of it, though, from many a source. My father was born in 1806, my grandfather in 1774, my great-grandfather in 1754, my great-great-grandfather in 1730, my great-great-great-grandfather in 1697, all on farms ; all were farmers, and the account of the old custom has been passed on. I have not heard of it during the past fifty-five years.

I regret very much the passing away of the old folk-lore and

50THE JOHN RYLANDS LIBRARY

legends of the past. On a winter's evening to sit around the old hearth-fire eating apples and drinking warm cider in the fitful light of the burning wood, and where the conversation became general, dulness did not take hold of the company, and tradition was passed on as in the old Icelandic Sagas.

How can we resuscitate English country life with all its old charms fast disappearing ?

Mr. Bond also draws my attention to the following passage in Hawkins' *History of Kingsbridge*, 1819, and shows that it is probably from Hawkins that Lysons obtained the tradition which we have quoted.

Hawkins, *loc. cit.*, pp. 71, 72 :—

" A custom of great antiquity prevails in these districts for the ciderist, on Twelfth Eve, attended by his workmen with a large can or pitcher of cider, guns charged with powder, etc., etc., to repair to the orchard, and there at the foot of one of the best bearing apple-trees drink the following toast three times repeated, discharging the firearms in conclusion :—

Here's to thee,
Old apple-tree,
Whence thou mayst bud,
And whence thou mayst blow,
And whence thou mayst bear
Apples enow,
Hats full !
Caps full !
Bushel bushel sacks full!
And my pockets full, too !
Huzza !

" The pitcher being emptied, they return to the house, the doors of which they are certain to find bolted by the females, who, be the weather what it may, are inexorable to all entreaties to open them till some one has divined what is on the spit which is generally a rarity not thought of, and, if edible, is the reward of him who first names it. The party are then admitted, and the lucky wight who guessed at the roast is recompensed with it."

ABERDEEN : THE UNIVERSITY PRESS

www.ingramcontent.com/pod-product-compliance
Lightning Source LLC
Chambersburg PA
CBHW021337290326
41933CB00038B/954